T0069122

Brassbones & Rainbows

The Collected Works of Shirley Bradley LeFlore

Foreword by
Amina Baraka

Introduction by
Gabrielle David

2LEAF PRESS

NEW YORK

www.2leafpress.org

P.O. Box 4378
Grand Central Station
New York, New York 10163-4378
editor@2leafpress.org
www.2leafpress.org

2LEAF PRESS
is an imprint of the
Intercultural Alliance of Artists & Scholars, Inc. (IAAS),
a NY-based nonprofit 501(c)(3) organization that promotes
multicultural literature and literacy.
www.theiaas.org

Copyright © 2013 by Shirley Bradley LeFlore
Cover art: Copyright © 2011 Frank Frazier
"Doo Wop Series: Those Sista's Can Sang"
Watercolor wash, 24" x 32"

Author Photo: Copyright © 2013 Kelly Revelle /
Revelle Photography, Crystal City, MO
www.revellephotography.com
Book design and layout: Gabrielle David

Library of Congress Control Number: 2013933086
BISAC: Poetry / American / African American
ISBN-13: 978-0-9884763-4-9 (Paperback)
ISBN-13: 978-0-9884763-8-7 (eBook)

10 9 8 7 6 5 4 3 2 1

Published in the United States of America

First Edition | First Printing

2LEAF PRESS trade distribution is handled by University of Chicago Press / Chicago
Distribution Center (www.press.uchicago.edu) 773.702.7010. Titles are also available for
corporate, premium, and special sales. Please direct inquiries to the UCP Sales Department,
773.702.7248.

All rights reserved. No part of this publication may be reproduced, stored in a retrieval
system, or transmitted in any form or by any means electronic, mechanical, photocopied,
recorded or otherwise without the prior permission of the Intercultural Alliance of Artists
& Scholars, Inc. (IAAS).

Dedicated to

my children, Hope, Jacie, and Lyah;
my grandchildren, Noelle, Jullian, Jordan
and Bella Grace

my now deceased parents, my sister Barbara,
my grandparents and extended family
that passed on the spirit of the creative arts
from a spiritual and cultural practice and perspective

CONTENTS

FOREWORD

THE POET SHIRLEY BRADLEY LEFLORE is a literary griot. Writing and telling stories, creating lyrics we can sing and dance to, she paints the lives of African American people through the eyes of a poet. Celebrating fifty years of being a literary composer, her blood runs blue, that of a survivor . . . .

Brassbones & Rainbows is a collage of Southern African American metaphors. In the first section, aptly titled, "Brassbones Reality," you can hear the music in the opening poem, "The Musician, for Julius Hemphill," and in "Saturdaynite Houserent," you can feel the characters come to life. Words dance off the page when you read "Singing the HooDoo Blues (haints on me)" and "Sonnybrotherman Dance," along with a number of homage poems found in this section. In "War—What is it Good For," the poems are dedicated to life, liberty, equality, justice and peace, which provoke deep and profound thought. "Rivers of Women" are lyrics made from love, drawn from strength and suffering, celebrating womanhood. It is here where you will find the poet's signature poems, "Rivers of Women" and "Illumination." "Rituals" the final section in this collection, rides the tide of "herstory" that touches on friendship, love, weddings and death. The poems are charged with an energy that continually explore what it's like to be female, what it's like to be a woman.

Shirley Bradley LeFlore uses language like Aretha Franklin sings notes: she writes things you can feel whether you read it or sing it out loud. *Brassbones & Rainbows* offers poems that breathe with words that burn. I urge you to read every single one.

Evolution-Revolution. �֍

— Amina Baraka
Newark, NJ
January 10, 2013

PREFACE

POETRY IS MY MUSE AND MY MUSIC, inspired by the social, spiritual, and political fabric of the human condition. I am profoundly moved by the spirit and sound of jazz, spirituals, blues, gospel and classical music.

It is important for me to recognize the cadre of musicians these poems have been performed with including the late Julius Hemphill, Oliver Lake, Bakida Carrol, Hamiet Bluiett, Floyd LeFlore and all of the outstanding BAG (Black Artists Group) musicians, poets, dancers, theater and visual artists. I want to give special recognition to J.D. Parran, who I worked with for many years, and to my good friend, singer Fontella Bass. I have worked with so many musicians, poets and other artists, it would be impossible to acknowledge them all.

I also want to mention those people who have specifically encouraged this publication, including Dorothy White, Ted Wilson, David Henderson, David Mills, Layding Kalib, Michael Castro, Eugene Redmond, K. Curtis Lyle, Marsha Cann, Charles Wartts, David Jackson, Zimbabwe Nkenya, David Parker and my editor, Deborah Mashibini. ✎

— Shirley Bradley Price LeFlore
St. Louis, Missouri
2012

INTRODUCTION

I AM VERY PROUD TO BE ASSOCIATED WITH the publication of Shirley Bradley LeFlore's first collection of poetry, *Brassbones & Rainbows*, a personal odyssey that successfully merges the familial seamlessly with the political, and the general woven with the homespun.

Shirley is an activist, performer, teacher, psychologist and mentor committed to using her skills as a writer not only to entertain, but also to educate and address historical, social and political issues in much of her poetry. Born and raised in St. Louis, Shirley is part of a literary tradition of African American women writers whose roots are firmly planted in the principles of feminism as well as a politicized ethnic identity. Her work has been published in literary journals and anthologies, and she has performed throughout the United States. She has also recorded CDs, and has appeared in numerous radio and television programs. In fact, few people know that Shirley was a key participant of the Civil Rights and Black Arts Movements during the 1960s and 1970s working closely with and establishing personal relationships with the likes of Margaret Walker, Gwendolyn Brooks and others. No stranger to the poetry community, Shirley is well-known, well-liked and well-respected, yet beyond this community, people know very little about her and her work.

Part of the reason she is not widely recognized is because Shirley has spent the better part of her nearly five decade career "doing" by focusing on teaching and giving. Rather than concentrating on self-promotion, she made what I believe was an unconscious effort to make a difference through personal connections that in the long run have had a tremendous impact on many people's lives, including my own. So while she has consistently written and performed great poetry over the years, she was unable to fully focus on writing and compiling what would have amounted to several poetry collections. Instead, raising a family, working on her degrees, teaching and working as a full-time performing artist were her priorities. After all of these years, the publication of *Brassbones & Rainbows* has been worth the wait. Untold hours of writing and years of studying the craft of poetry have culminated into one of the finest debut collections I've seen to date.

Brassbones & Rainbows is centered on Shirley's life including tributes to some of the people she has met along the way. Growing up in St. Louis, a city that has a long history of African American artistic excellence, Shirley was exposed to "an intelligent home" that encouraged her to "listen to different things." Besides creating and performing plays and dances in the backyard, she often listened to her mother recite poetry, or hung out in the kitchen while her grand-parents, aunts and uncles shared stories about their family, or delved into spir-ited conversations about the political and social issues of the day. Her love for literature grew while attending public school, where she discovered the likes of Daniel Defoe (the author of *Robinson Crusoe*) and poets Paul Laurence Dunbar and Langston Hughes. In time, Shirley found herself writing poetry as a mode of inquiry and response. It would become a means of sounding out and awakening the spirit of her community through ideas and art.

One can only imagine that while Shirley sat in the kitchen listening to her family members trade stories, a new kind of music wafted throughout her home. It was the 1950s and St. Louis blues was being joined by a new sound: R&B, which evolved out of the jump blues of the late 1940s—with St. Louisans Ike and Tina Turner at the forefront. Throw in jazz innovator Miles Davis at the be-ginning of his career in nearby East St. Louis (Illinois) and those weekly church services Shirley had to attend every Sunday, and it's no surprise how music became an important foundation to her incredibly powerful poetry.

But perhaps one of the most important components of Shirley's poetry is that "doing" part I mentioned earlier, which fermented during the social activ-ism of the 1950s. When a revitalized NAACP in St. Louis, under Ernest Cal-loway's presidency, launched a mass offensive against the entire edifice of Jim Crow and de facto racism with vigorous civil disobedience campaigns, a teen-aged Shirley joined the NAACP Youth Group and participated in sit-ins and marches. As "Civil Rights" segued to "Black Power" in the mid-to-late 1960s, the black political landscape became more fractured and conflict-ridden, one that quickly evolved into a battleground of competing ideologies. In the midst of this revolution, St. Louis quickly was transformed into a meeting point between the Black Arts Movement of the South and the Midwest.

Active in the theater and literary arts communities during the late 1960s, Shirley jumped into the thick of it as a member of the Black Artists Group (BAG), an artistic collective committed to a collaborative interweaving of di-verse artistic mediums. This collective, which consisted of musicians, writers and artists such as Oliver Lake, Hamiet Bluiett, J.D. Parran and Malinké Elliott, contributed to the cultural richness of St. Louis and created a strong model for inter-artistic cooperation and arts-driven social activism. By the time BAG petered out in 1972, Shirley was already pursuing her Bachelor's degree in Be-havioral Science and Language Arts, and would later receive her Masters degree in Psychology in 1981. In time, she would combine science and writing into a curriculum that would build her reputation as a Professor of Psychology who uniquely utilized language arts; and as a Professor of English and Creative Writ-ing specializing in African American and women's literature at numerous col-leges and universities in Missouri. She would also travel around the country, especially to New York, to perform, lecture and hold workshops. For a change of pace, in 1990 Shirley moved to New York to teach in New York City, New Jersey and Vermont. Although she returned to St. Louis in 1996 to continue teaching, she frequently visited New York.

Actually, it was during one of those visits that I met Shirley in 1998 at Steve Cannon's Gathering of the Tribes in Loisada. She was promoting the CD, *Spirit Stage,* a musical-poetry collaboration she recorded with J.D. Parran, Warren Smith, Stephen Haynes, Bill Ware, Brad Jones, Joan Bouise, Tony Cedras and Kelvyn Bell. In fact that night, she performed "Put'cha Haints on Me" with J.D. and blew the house down! When the poet Tony Medina introduced me to Shirley, it sparked the beginning of our literary collaboration, from bookings at the Langston Hughes Community Library co-producing television programs and participating as a board member of our organization to the publication of this remarkable book.

An underlying characteristic of much of Shirley's work consists of socially conscious verse influenced by feminist activism. Like many nascent feminists of the times such as Maya Angelou, Joy Harjo, Adrienne Rich and Audre Lorde, Shirley always understood that in order to thrive—not just survive—women must learn how to adapt to society's ever-changing rhythms without sacrificing their own identities in the process. And with the effortless musicality of her language, Shirley never assumes a static definition of the African American woman, but rather, always challenges readers to think about what it means to be "American," "black," and "woman" at different historical moments in our lives.

Shirley writes with an imagination of the senses by using wonderful metaphorical language, which is probably why she has spent an incredible amount of time culling these poems. The verses flow in an easy going, smooth and soothing Southern American dialect mixed with African American Vernacular English—its intensity changing from poem to poem—with words serving as musical notes. She opens *Brassbones & Rainbows* with the poem, "The Musician," which begins with a beauty of a line: "There's a man singing under my skin." Not only is it mind-blowing, it's actually an appropriate introduction to this collection since Shirley's metaphors succeed in getting under our skin, making us smile with wonderment as her words roll off our tongues.

Brassbones & Rainbows is presented in four sections: (1) "Brass Reality," (2) "War—What is it Good for," (3) "Rivers of Women" and (4) "Rituals." In the first section, "Brass Reality," Shirley shapes the direction of her recounted memories of her childhood with a searing and raw honesty that carries the reader. One standout is "Singing the HooDoo Blues (haints on me)":

> "Put'cha haints on me /
> Put summa dat goobie dus alroun my feet
> Pluck a lock of mah hair—wear it ever'where
> Wring a chick'ns neck til it hoop
> Sprinkle seasalt / under mah stoop

Criss cross me wld a blk catz bone
Lawd lawd make me wanna stay home" (p. 21).

Shirley also writes about poets Amiri Baraka, Eugene Redmond and responds to
Maya Angelou's *I Know Why The Caged Bird Sings*.

"War—What is it Good For," a phrase from the Edwin Starr song from the
1960s sung during protests against the Vietnam War, begins with the mind-war
played on the people who perished in Guyana in 1978, and jumps from street
justice, to 9/11, to Dr. King, showing how war comes to us in many guises. Listen
to Shirley tell us about 9/11 in "State of Emergency":

"blue-nite lite up the morning sky
w/unsettled passion exploding between
steel cobalt legs screaming
across the sun two long purple tears running down" (p. 43).

or "Dream/eaters":

"dream/eaters on the edge
broken like glass/on the edge
they wear no mask/just the wind
they are the bloodrunners/on the edge
they swallow the stars/chew up the moon
light up the air after dark / on the edge
they are the war/unlisted soldiers / they are our battlescars
on the edge/edging" (p. 37).

The third section of *Brassbones & Rainbows*, "Rivers of Women," contains
most of Shirley's women poems, which cover a wide range of subjects includ-
ing self-identity, inner-strength, beauty, love and faith. Included in this section
is Shirley's signature poem, "Rivers of Women": "I HAVE KNOWN WOM-
EN/RIVERS OF WOMEN /blu/blck/tan/high/yella/blu-vein wom-
en/rivercrossing women . . ." (p. 53). Beautiful lines abound in this section, like
"across bloodline and geography / the women gather/coming in from their
winter / threads of yesterday's fabric / like a tattered dress that once/danced
adult circle ..." ("Broken N' Parts," p. 57); or "With long enchanting fingers
she kisses the deep blue / lips of sound melting into every string . . ." ("Il-
lumination," p. 62); or a gospel tribute to Mahalia Jackson: "I woke up this
morning / More than something on my mind / Woke up/Under a New Or-
leans sky" ("My Soul Looks Back in Wonder 'How I Got Over'," p. 63); or "I
house the legend Mutima /The heartbeat of the earth/I am the offspring of
the moon and the sun/Thrust from energy of Africa / I am the Black Woman"
("Poem for a Black Woman," p. 69).

The last section of this collection, "Rituals," explores everyday things; the healing of visible scars or invisible wounds, family gatherings, tributes to family and friends who have "crossed over into the hush" ("Rider of the Tide," p. 81). In the poems "A Tribute to the Ancestors" (p. 86) and "Family Re/union," Shirley emphasizes the importance of family. Here is what she says in "Family Re/union":

> We come
> Gathering across geographies
> Knitting hands/blending heartbeats
> A melody in unison/ a harmonic convergence
> Celebrating the breathprints of our bloodline
> Stringing the gift of love like gospel pearls
> Around our waist (p. 87).

Throughout this collection, Shirley blends realism with lyricism, interspersed with humor, and then takes it one step further by accurately depicting the lives of common, everyday people (most of them women) with vivid imagery. These relatively short and accessible poems with allusions to black culture and music are surprisingly synaptic. The poems connect to each other because they are all drawn from a lifetime of living that affirms the strength and fragility of the long-term ties of kinship, as well as the joys and pleasures set against the real possibility of disappointment and loss. More importantly, Shirley's poems are generally suffused by a keen sense of the ideal and by a profound love of humanity, especially toward African Americans.

Shirley's work succeeds because she is a storyteller, or rather, a story *singer*. She uses language to continue our oldest tradition of gifting the tale, sharing the fabric of verse through sound, creating poetic lines into phrases of jazz and blues, from the lyrical to the polemical. For Shirley, the "personal," the "political" and the "poetical" are indissolubly linked, and her body of work can be read as a series of urgent dispatches from the front. Many of her titles, such as "Saturdaynite Houserent" (p. 11), "Singing the HooDoo Blues (haints on me)" (p. 21), and "When a Sisterwomenpoet Prays" (p. 56), sing their own brief tales, with her poems becoming a breathing living artifice that jumps off the page, begging to be sung out loud more than once.

In this long-awaited debut collection, Shirley proves that she is a true griot who values her role as "Poet." What *Brassbones & Rainbows* accomplishes is that it showcases an innovative writer who has been left out of too many critical discussions because she did not match the popular paradigm of her era. Let's just hope that after all these years, Shirley will finally receive the recognition she deserves, from poetry aficionados, students of poetry, and the many remarkable generations of women writers to come. ❀

— Gabrielle David
New York City
February 24, 2013

Brassbone Reality

The Musician
for *Julius Hemphill*

There's a man singing under my skin

Like a gourd song
With a clear voice
Singing the silk of a hummingbird
Deepthroat in the silverblades of holygrass

There's a man singing under my skin

Like a drumchoir
Wind/jamming my bluespots
Blowing the dust off my wings
Sifting the texture of my nature
Rich and mahogany
B'tween long enchanting fingers
Plucking out my ruptured nerve
Restringing me

There's a man singing under my skin

Like a brassband
Breast stroking my winds
Moving with a bebop/eye
Scattin on these haints
Charming these cooties
Putting some rhythm on these bluenotes
Swinging low on a sweet chariot
Making my spirit rise
Jamming jazzing jamming
Like a poet chewing on a sonnet
Rearranging my score

This singing man is dancing under my skin

With easyfeet
To a metronome stride
Dancing a full scale
With an insatiable passion

This man with a boogie / woogie ear
Layin down a gypsy / string bassline in brass
Sundancing me gold like a Mississippi yam
This man moving like a congo / waltz
Doing the bambooli and a hoochie / coo

This man singing & dancing / under my skin

With a whole sahara of tambourines
Stringing a gospel / pearl between my haints and my harmony
Between my rapture and my rupture
Reconnecting my muscles, my nerves, my bones
With a soprano tongue
Turning my brassbones to rainbows

This man / this singing / this dancing
Under my skin has broken my silence

out / loud

Saturdaynite Houserent

saturday nite and the lites are low
the music is loud and the lovin is slow

possum got tators and the coon got gravy
crowders in the pot and i like mine hot

come on round to the back of my flat
open the door when i throw the latch

you can't be jivin when the lites flick on
cause we got some juju and a barr'l of corn

betty and mable and marylu,
e.j. and willie gon be there too,

dice'll be rollin big pearl be callin,
if your luck ain't good you can still be ballin

cause short dress chics and big apple dudes
be gittin down with the hoochie coo

look out for shortee and his 45
with anniemae glued to his side

he gon start showin out trying to be cool
watch him dare harvey to step on his shoes

check clothilde when she gets real loud
and screams on Leroy "git your hand from under my dress
fore i git my razor and sample your chest"

muddywaters be duelin with memphis slim
whil lit'nin hopkins and howlin wolf be waitin to take over again

you can look for hattiemae to get real hi
and her ole man curtis gon be peepin sly out the corner of his eye
to make sure juanita gon be standin by

dorothy's gon commence to pullin up her dress
and roosevelt gon have to give her some fist to make her rest

way in the background, cutting thru the noise,
sarah's gon be scattin *sho bop de du sha ba be du* dattin
and big daddy fats gon sho nuf be cattin

yeh — soulville baby at the gloryhole
put your chump change in your pocket
park your coup de ville and lock it

saturday nite and the lites are low
the music is loud and the lovin is slow

possums got tators and the coon got gravy
crowders in the pot and i like mine hot....

Rayboy Blk & Bluz
ode to Arthur R. Brown

I rememba
Rayboy blu / blk bug-eyed wid yo chocolate smile
when you wuz jus knee-hi to a hoppergrass
and time was 1 / 2 pass a monkey's ass
memba — when you wuz jus a lil scuttle-butt / jr. flip
hip-dipped in the mouth of the south
tongue pluckin cotton in the Mississippi bottoms

Memba — you sittin roun' yo granddaddies ankles
eye suckin his footprints — soppin yo history like a
biscuit doing gravy — collectin yo shadows — sharpenin yo wings
on the teeth of yo ancestors — tuckin them words in yo hip-pocket
w / yo chocolate smile and yo lil boogie-bugle
you wuz passin-off for a trumpet

I rememba
Rayboy blu / blk and bug-eyed
when them white sheets lit up the night like toe-jam fever
when yo dadddie did a two fisted nigga-knuckle dance
on a crackers ass and in less than 3 days he was pushin up daisies and
underneath tha ole Magnolia tree the low-dixie wind
wuz whistling a breeze around that old rugged burnt out cross
and yo momma's tears wuz proud mary

I rememba
you playin on yo 2 string guitar in the out-house
when you swore on a capone and a rooster that someday
you wuz gonna take Gabriel to a duel befo that great gittin-up morning
said you wuz gona take him down solo / so low said you
wuz gona smack him w / a vamp and then snatch one of yo poems
outcha lil-hip pocket and word-whoop him to death
wid yo good-foot strong as red-devil lye and dare him to rise

I rememba — memba
when you said you wuz gona git-up / fly right and do
a lite foot and hummin shuffle, git on that Rock Island Line
that side-winds at the junction roun-midnite / said you wuz gon
put some dust between you and them death-hounds breath'n
on yo heels / said you wannit to blow-blast some real brass

do a shu-shu / bop-hop wid yo hip lip and / a rebop vamp / do a rap
so boss that it mess-up a wet dream and make a cockroach sing

I rememba — you
Rayboy blu / blk bug-eyed wid yo chocolate smile
O yeh, o yeh — I remember.

Sonnybrotherman Dance

Hey, sonnybrother dance
Get down, Get down
Get up, Get up
Dance sonnybrotherman dance
Go on back in time — show it to us
Your time
Times time
That smiled and cried
And laughed and worked
And peed all over you
Dance with the bet you made with time

Sonnybrotherman dance

Dance a conga — a watch and a chain
Dance a toothstardiamond
Squared and set in gold
Go on and dance a biscuit-toe stroll

Dance a cotton field / a tobacca farm
A steelmill grind / on a watermelon rind
Dance a bowlegged-pigeontoed
Slufooted dude
And don't forget to dance
Forty acres and a mule

Dance Sonnybrotherman dance

Dance a Mandance
Dance that boy named colored down in the ground
Stomp that boy named nigga with your 200 pound
Dance that name deep
Real sweet
Dance a grand dance — A man dance
A man Dance, a man Dance, A man Dance

Dance Sonnybrotherman dance

Tell the world
You done earned your board and keep
Tell 'em from rite there in your feet

Dance Sonnybrotherman dance

Time done sprinkled goobie-dust all round your bed
Done tried to run you naked crazy clean out your head

Dance an ole dance
        a new dance
            its the same dance

Dance a boggie-woogie, jitterbug
The jack and the ball
The camel walk — the lindy-hop
A little taste of be-bop,
The rag, the slow drag
The cake walk — a little sand slide
Try a little bit of the boody-grind
Don't worry bout the choking-kind
Do the hukka-buck, chug-alug
The slop, the stroll, and if that ain't enouf
You can try the jelly-roll

Dance sonnybrotherman dance

You don paid your dues
Work a lil soft shoe
Dance your own tune
Cuz you the one that gave
Birth to the blues — not Frank Sinatra

Dance a man dance, a hand dance, a land dance
Dance Sonnybrotherman Danzzz...

East Eye Rider

for Eugene B. Redmond

East-eye rider
Mounts his river boots
Ready to see-ride & roll the walls of the Mississippi
Stone rolling & wading beyond
Searching the crouch of the river-griot
Snatching the root-books & water-scrolls
Dusting them like chaffing off the wind
Gathering the kneecaps of wisdom-reapers & river-juju

       Ready to sing

East-eye rider
With a seed sack strapped to his hip-bone
Full of the footprints of river-runners
Black as the mahogany nite / deep as a muddywater bluz
Moving with the flow ripe as the gold of yams when the sun strikes
With a satchel full of spirits / ancestor spirits / spirits of legends / legions of spirits
Moving on spirits / survivors of the cross spirits / life spirits

       Ready to sow

East-eye rider
With a born again wind in his lungs
With the word like fist clenched between his teeth
Double-clutchin on a single note
Eyeballing our path / our road / our journey
Tracking and collecting / storehousing our stories
Smoothing out the wrinkle
Pen-lickin the wounds of our lacerated story
Sanctifying the heroes and sheroes of the lost ark
Picture-framing our name / preserving our images
East-eye rider
Wordwalker of our age / cultural sage
E'negue, Bodacious
He'z fire on the water
Keeping us smoking

Poets Muse
for Amiri Baraka

he comes w / Afrosonic feet / wordwalking
like a baritone saxamony sonnet movin
underskin / be-boppin / boogiebluzinin
the free-word order / giant-talkin tongue

jammin / stirring the souls of black folk
busting the kneecaps of the american
nightmare / undressing the people of the lie
w / the naked truth / callin nigganauts

out of orbit n'2 consciousness / spirithouse
keeper / BARAKA FIRE / keeps comin–poet
unplugged & plugged in

Brass Reality
dedicated to Lester Bowie

BADDASSBRASSMANBOWIE / snatched the wind from b'tween
    the legs of your ancestors / recycling their tongues
    hijacking their breathprints / giving voice
    to their spirit / screamin like a cathound spread eagle
    hummin in the throat of a silver trumpet / singing
    like a silk sardine talking back to god

    up above my head I hear the musik / reclaiming you
    up above my head I hear the musik / reaffirming you

    restringing your nerves / your bones like a sanctified
    sonnet / rebirthing the morning / up above my head
    I hear the musik

BRASSMANBOWIE / your musik like innerlight in a blindman's vision
    innersighting our 3rd ear so we can hear the light in the heartbeat
    of the darkbluz — people harmonizing the night
    dancing freedom a passageway / into the light / into the sun / into
       the rising / like
    your musik rising LESTER / keep rising LESTER /
    keep dancing with the night LESTER / rocksteady
    dancin wid dem rocks / rollin em like the musik

BADDASSBRASSMANBOWIE / bringing in the morning / bringing up the light
    so we can keep hearing the musik / so we can keep dancing
    life b'tween these brassbones and rainbows

    up above my head I can hear the musik

    and remember / a holler from the hills / the word from the field
    from a blackmouth hand singing on a cottonseed & sucking on the wind
    I hear you singing a reach back trying time solo

    you can bury me in the east
    you can bury me in the west
    but I'm gonna rise-up and be a TRUMPET in the mawnin*............*

* *negro spiritual*

Bird Caged

the caged bird always sings
god gave it a song and six wings
a firesong
last time and the next time too
a firesong, burning for joy
yearning for peace
firesong, struggling for food and shoes
begging nomore dues that don't ever get paid
the caged bird always sings
black crow-caws like a mocking bird's repeat
o-hear freedom ring—far in a distant

anybody know what bird be caged

cagedbird be black as the color of some truelove's hair
but it got wings
it got eyes that cry in the wilderness, "feed the sparrows"
but it got wings
cagedbird be real in lifebooks that don't ever get read
but it got wings
the bird looks back 400 years and sees 400 years hence
and screech, jesus wuz a man just like my daddy
and sometimes my mamma
bird be colored ibo-ebony, sundawnbronze and a tallered yellow
with a black grandma

the cagedbird always sings
god gave it a song and six wings
the bird just wants to trade freedoom for freedom
sing its song and use its six wings

> i got 2 wings to cover my face
> 2 wings to cover my feet
> & 2 wings to fly away*

*negro spiritual

Singing the HooDoo Blues
(haints on me)

Put'cha haints on me
Put summa dat goobie dus alroun my feet
Pluck a lock of mah hair — wear it ever'where
Wring a chick'nz neck til it hoop
Sprinkle seasalt / under mah stoop
Criss cross me wid a blk catz bone
Lawd lawd make me wanna stay home

>   Sorcerize me if you must
>   Work yo roots sho-nuf
>   Cuz I like the way you do my stuff

Ya makes my juice box run
Lik hot butter'd rum
Ya love me so good
I wanna skip jump & run
Makes me def blind & dumb

Put'cha haints on me
Squeeze me lik ya do that eagle on a dolla
Take ma whisper to a holla /
Turn ma minutes to an hour/
Increase me to the 3rd power

Put'cha haints on me

>   Sorcerize me if ya must
>   Work ya roots sho nuf
>   Cuz I like the way you do yr stuff

When you see me comin / click ya heels 3 times
Wid a grigri rhyme / but dontcha make no wish
When ya see me comin / beat ya breast 3 times
And make a mojo sign / but dontcha make no wish
B'cause ya fix won't mix/ on a Creole woman fish

Gon & put'cha haints on me

Now, ya kin snake hip me and tare up ya face
Ya know I lov being yo amazing grace

So re nu me do me wid ya hoodoo bluz
Wid a hex ana spell
an sum duji ju ju

Gon & put'cha haints on me

I won't burn no candle drink no frog-eye tea
Put no bunkleberry leaves up my sleeves.
Kiss my elbow or hoot oil my knees
I won't bathe in no sage
carry no cloves for 3 days
And I won't search for no conjure man wid no lousanna hand
To take em off

Jus rememba who you dowhenyoudodahoodoo
Cuz you may be tha who/who be hoodoo'd

Lightfoot & Hummin

I hear you comin
Lightfoot and hummin
Like an uptown blues
Wearing them woreout downtown shoes

I hear you
Like a rock rolling stonesmooth
Checking out the vibes — eyeballing the signs
Trying to see blind

I hear you comin
Lightfoot and hummin
W/ a windcharming angel folded under your wings
Some leftover dreams — the earth folkdancin, circling your feet

I hear you
Silent like night & easy like evening
Strumming your pain like a stringmissin guitar
Guarding your star

I hear you comin
Songwalking me w/a leconic sound
Eyepicking my waters like a juice harp
Trying to play me

I hear you
Moonstroking me like gold
Sipping off my city soul
Musing the soft in my bend
But a countryriver woman ain't got no end

I hear you comin
Lightfoot & hummin
Like a hush hush hobo
Working your boogie-juggie mojo

I hear you
I hear you comin
Lightfoot & hummin

Now you can go on 'bout your bizness

Quietstorm

He
Came by night
Moved inside me
With a pocket/full of rainbows

He
Came with the holy/ghost
To chase the devil away
Walked like hieroglyphics
Thru my temple

He came
Writing the psalms of ancient pyramids
On the walls of my soul
Singing a 2000 year old anthem
Making me song

He came
A soft-sculpturer designing still / visions
Draped my body velvet
Stretched me out on a canvas
Of cool waters

He came
Speaking in tongues to my spirit
Crested a star in my forehead
Sealed it with his sign
Moved his sun around my moon

Made the rains gather at the river
Of my thighs
And my navel full
With sacred oil
Giving birth
To a real love ritual

He came
To baptize my history
Purge my future

He
Came by night
        a quietstorm

use/ta/be

I cd sing of memories
and once upon a time
and
tender
tht cross'd my heart
and
eyes
and
use to be sighs
tht cried
b'tween
my thighs
and laid hands on my mind
and
kept me hi
naturally
but/but/but
I
wd only
b
reminded
of
u
gone w/ the wind ....

Love Poem

I am a love poem
let me be

I am not light
I am not heavy
I am neither rite nor wrong
jus consider me
the balance

I sit low in the corner of your left eye
see inside the depth of high in your right
I stand in the center of space
confirm the substance of time

I am a love poem
let me be

I am tired
of your lamenting
tired of you trying to direct my course
falsely accusing me, explaining me, blaming me
for your own short comings
and to be very frank
I am tired of you always trying to kill yourself in my name
I am for the living
call me love

you assault me,
throw me against stonewalls, stomp on me,
maul me with your knees
squash me between your toes
spit on me
then say
love is painful

you insult me
put me down—shake me down
call me weak
starve me like hungry
let me go naked
walk on my rhythm
then say
love is cruel

you forbid
I visit your children's eyes
kiss their heart
watch over them
to keep the evil spirits away
you uninvite me to your weddings
absent me from your lovemaking
deny my comfort in your deaths
in your partings and bindings
between friendship and kinships
then say
love has no compassion

you have the nerve
to take my name in vain
on most occasions
having no intentions
of lettin me be

I am a love poem
gathered 2'gether in my own name

I move with precision
yet I move freely
I bear no chains
yet I am the link
I am not forceful
yet I am force
I am energy
I am beauty
when you learn of my ways

I move with both feet flat on the earth
spreadeagle in midair
kiss the mouth of the heavens
I am constant in strength
the source of understanding
God's seed

I am a love poem
gathered 2'gether in my own name

so pick me up from amongst all your broken glass
and let me be

Men

for Lorenzo Pace, painter

Men have buttered my bread on both-sides
Wined me, dined me
Took me to the ball
Loved me like Sunday morning church
Glory all the week
Bathed me in sunshine
Almost melted me blind
Touched me gently with their minds
Laid hands on my soul
Some lasted thru the cold
Coming full circle in July

Men have buttered my bread on both-sides
Wined me, dined me
Took me to the ball
Some flew me around their world
1/2 inch short of getting back to my own
Laid hands on my secrets
Made my nature high
My temperature rise
Turned my whisper to a scream
Made me holler, *please!*
And laugh between my knees
Some fried me, tried me, burned me
Washed me, wrung me, hung me out to dry
Some disappeared, left me tripping, tipping into darkness
Some sent me to the school of hard knocks, rocks in my bed
That almost settled in my head

Men have buttered my bread on both-sides
They have revived me, saved me, soothed me, renewed me,
Refreshed my memories
Made pain jump back off my joy
All in a 1/2 split second
Saved my natural born life

Men have buttered my bread on both sides
Wined me, dined me
Took me to the ball—showed me life the paradise/life the paradox
But they still be
My sweet inspirations

Let a Poet Blk Sing

when a poet blk sings

they don't trip off the fantasy-but create real creations
w / new images — refresh drybones rising
scream like a bird on a fence
        (don't cha kill em)
they soul be wired to electrify, sanctify
and speak to you in a new tongue older than age

let a poet blk sing

they be the life searchers
the earth scratchers
w / the blood of strange fruit under their fingers
they itch and itch to get rid of the bitch
that won't let they people go
lifting their pen & voice
they bring yesterdaze into today and redefine tomorrow
they be the heartbeat of their ancestors
firespitters who split lies and let truth be
        (they be the revelators of time)

let a poet blk sing

a planted by the water song
that shall not be moved
but moves to reach — to touch — to get to you
they want to lay your burden down
teach you to study wars and rumors of wars
until there be no more wars

let a poet blk sing

a life song, a death dirge
jam like a birdman charlie vamp
whose sound broke the limb of the hangman's tree
they write for the hot train that carried coltranes strain
into a sweet melody
to eulogize a bessie
to bless a billie

transcend a dinah
the freebirds of paradise
made captive
who left hell lifting up they eyes
like music
bittersweet tone with the savinggrace power
to vindicate and emancipate
a you, me, us into weusi all the way home

let a poet blk sing

of frustration for the bloods flood
who be rushin their volcano eruption
a song for the youth
a praise for the old
they pray for the rainbow — not the sign — resurrect hope

so
get back   o mississippi
                muddy mississippi
                bloody mississippi
                o redriversea of my father's bones
                o redriversea of my mother's flesh

get back o scarlet harlot
o redneck yellowbelly mississippi

                and let

a poet blk sing

                rolling like Jordan ....

War – What is it Good for

Guayana Suite 1978

I (The People)

10,000 souls were fed
arsenic and ole lace
found them dead

they came
the wanderers
seeking from stranger to stranger
door to door
they knocked
petitioners of the bleeding hearts
n search of self
while self stood naked, wide awake
n'side the sleep of their soul's temple

10,000 souls were fed
arsenic and ole lace
found them dead

these were they
who waited/who prayed
in the shadow of their me-ism
but they did not watch

these were they
who waited/who prayed
  for the sign
  for the voice
  the messiah
  the allah
  the jehova
  the buddah
  the hoodoo guru
    but they did not watch

II (The Prophet)

let us gather 2'gether in my name
2'gether cum
for the laying on of hands
he came

a voice not crying in the wilderness — jus the wild-ness
saying
I am the sign
I am the lite
the prophet (profit)
the shepherd-keeper of the sheep

cuz I got a gee-zus complex

saying
bring me your aged
bring me your youth
cum when terror runneth at your heels
cum when your stars have burned holes in your hopes
cum when your fantasies have frantasised
and your dreams deferred

cuz I got a gee-zus complex

a song for your singin
a prayer for your prayin
a sermon for your surrender

he came
10,000 souls were fed
arsenic and ole lace
found them dead

III (The Passage)
at the fountain
their cups were filled
rites were read
stone to hard
sand too quick
and sister caroline sang a grayswansong

there was no eulogy
no ritual
jus a box recycled, with a bag of ole bones
aged too cold
beneath the hymnal I heard
the long lonesigh / a shortquietwhisperdrone

drank, yes I did
why not, I was tired of waitin for geezus
never you mind
I know'd it wasn't him
so, don't sing me no grayswansong sista caroline
save it for the youngins

stone too hard
sand too quick
and sister caroline sang a grayswansong

there was no eulogy
no ritual
jus a box recycled
I heard
a passing over moan
I was just amongst the multitude who were fed
giving my tomorrow away
now standin' in the need of a grayswansong
and I can't hear ya sister caroline

there was another voice familiar to all time
I too did drink, I was always scared,
always a marcher / always joinin
lookin for myself /
when he said he cared
it seemed so sweet — I jus wanted a little peace

stone too hard
sand too quick
and sister caroline sang a grayswansong
thus be the eulogy
the ritual

a small box rattled, a clean almost clear
soundless noise between a whisper and a whimper
the bones clattered n'side the stillness,
a child's mute voice
I drank
but I never wanted to
I tol mama
my becoming had not yet come

my dreams curdled on my stomach
my breath sucked my chance on tomorrow
for it was to be my generation who was to discover the mission
for it was my freedom to rise in my climbing or fall in my failing
and mama, I didn't get a chance to kiss grandma, hug daddie or
say goodbye to uncle duke

so sister caroline please sing me a grayswansong and color it rainbow
paint it sunshine with a scarlet brush
for me and my lit'l sista sparky
cuz we are the ones of those chosen who were
gathered 2'gether in no name

stone too hard
sand too quick
and sister caroline sang a grayswansong

let time do the gathering of souls
in the palm of the wind
and speak peace to our spirit
the children comin unto you

10,000 souls were fed
arsenic and ole lace
found them dead
the old
the scattered
the innocent

Dream/eaters

dream/eaters on the edge
broken like glass/on the edge
they wear no mask/just the wind
they are the bloodrunners/on the edge
they swallow the stars/chew up the moon
light up the air after dark/on the edge
they are the war/unlisted soldiers/they are our battlescars
on the edge/edging

they celebrate their own "rights of passage"
avenging their ancestors
the revenge of the middle-passage This is edging time

they confuse the just w/just-us
no Justice/Just-ice Edging

dream/eaters on the edge, smoking dreams/on the edge
stompin dreams/on the edge
you can smell them before daybreak/
spoiled before ripe/on the edge
see their shadows at high-noon/on the edge

they suck eyes/on the edge...sweet eyes/bitter eyes/innocent
eyes/stone eyes/ free & easy eyes/elder eyes/dodo eyes/
bitch eyes — they suck eyes with angry straws/on the edge
eyesuckin/dream/eaters/on the edge
w/wet-soggy dreams/on the edge

in the street/on the edge
in the hot arms of a funky-beat/on the edge
they die & die & die & die/on the edge
they have no winding sheet/no coolinboard they just die
w /no medals/no honor/backs against their tomorrows
unborn/on the edge they die
with just one crystal teardrop
trapped in the echo of a mother's scream STOOOPPPPP!

This Poem

This is a spirit poem
Beating my breast like a drum
Talking up a storm
Coming hooploop and crazyhorse
Painting Red-Cloud and Black Elk
Singing Geronimo
Speaking the great-tongue of
Earthmother Rainbow
Listening to skywalkers pray
For Leonard Peltier
Wounded in the knee and heart
With the waterbuffalo spreadeagle

This is a spirit poem
Doing a flashback

When the mountain carried a windsong
In its bosom
And the valley cradled the footprints of god
And bird / beast / field / flower / man and sky were family
Before my trail of tears

This is a spirit poem
Doing a flashback

Before the terrorists came
Humpedback and foothoofed
Riding ironhorse with the taste of power
In their lefthand
Foaming at the mouth and a killing / eye

A spirit poem / a poem w / a memory
Doing a flashback

Beating the hell out of truth
With a sack full
Of tricks and treaties
Signed in blood and lies
And peace broken like glass

A spirit poem/a poem w/ a memory
Doing a flashback

Singing squawstealing and bloodmixing
With nature moaning menred
Dead with feathers in their head
On reservations and rations

This is a spirit poem/doing a flashback
Before the terrorists came

This is a spirit poem
Beating my breast like a drum
Hot like juju

A sweatin/soulin poem

Dragging swansongs and silence like night
Dragging rusted chains w/ no grace
Pulling the weepin and wailin
Thru the middle passage
Like billows rolling and breakers dashing
Thru muddywaters bloody
Once gold like yams

A sweaten/soulin poem

With screaming in the eye
Rocking and rolling time
Of renegades and runaways and
The Arkansas brownskin soldiers
Copper/eyes and licorice feet
Purple faces / nutmeg hands
In a desperate land
Sheetwrapped Klan
Knees scarred and circles broken

A sweatin / soulin poem

A hangin poem/a raping poem
A court and elder poem
A charging poem

Charging terrorist and thieves
With stolen property / stolen birthrights
And people and dreams and visions
Choking saints w / jesus in a gunnysack

This is a spirit poem w / a memory
Doing a flashback

Talking about shingles and shit / true grit
And grime and dirty hearts and hands
Like pimps playing GOD and NASTY
On the smoothgreen of capitol hill
While the people pay the bill

This is a spirit poem SCREAMNNNNNN
                    in your face

WAR / WHAT FOR ?????????????
Hiroshima / Vietnam / Grenada / El Salvador /
Nicaragua / Panama / South Africa / Mississippi /
Middle East / Alabama / Chicago / Iraq / A / MERRI / CA

A screaming poem
For the hungry / the homeless / diseased / dis-eased
Violence / violins and Ola Mae's babies

A screamin poem

Heaving in my bosom
Knocking on my tombstone
Hailing Mary / weeping and wailing
Yelling and screaming
A breakdown and rappin poem

SCREAMINNNN — in ya face

This is a Spirit Poem
A today poem
Doing a drumcall / drumtalking in word walkin
In rhythm and sometimes rhyme
Calling men / women / children
With short eyes / wrinkled wrists twisted ankles lips and hearts
Wringing like ole dirty dishrags

This is a today poem / a callin poem
To break the yoke of lies
And be blessed

A woman calling poem to walk in grace
Thru her storm, suck up the light drink
Fresh water take her place in the sun
And be healed

A man calling poem to rise up make his bed
Gather his loins / his courage /
His babies / his women
And be healed

A children calling poem to smother the anger of their nowness
Soak-up the sunshine of their newness feel the power
Of their dreams / their vision & see all the good inside / sing
A lovesong for their tomorrows unborn
And be healed

Calling the prophets / the preacher / the priest / politician
Physician to be healed

This is a today poem / a callin poem / a healing poem
To break the yoke of the people of the lie
To be blessed poem

This is not a revelation poem
But a revolution poem
Because revolutions are born
Out of the evolution of every
Generation

This poem may never be heard
But it will keep on hearing
This poem may never be seen
But it will keep on seeing

SO DON'T TRY TO KILL THIS POEM
JUST KEEP WRITING
                    THIS POEM ....

War—What is it Good For

Weeping knows no borders / Blood knows no borders / Death
Knows no borders

The Dead / the Mangled & Maimed / the Innocent / the Guilty
Will still be the Dead / the Mangled & Maimed / the Innocent / the Guilty

There is no good war
War never ejaculates peace

Only the babies w/ no weapons / the mothers trying to hide
Their children under their skirt / and untrodden dust trails runnin
Blood and skin and bones / and bombs BOOM BOOM BOOM
Killing has no borders no winners / no losers

The dead / the mangled & maimed / the innocent / the guilty /
Are still dead / mangled & maimed / innocent / guilty

War —what is it good for?   BOOM!

Oil / Land / Money / Power and the tired ole men with paper mache visions
That kill the dreams of the young ones sent into harm's way
With the promise of life — BOOM BOOM — destroyed in a day /
An hour / a minute / old men festering with power and push
Button pride — saving face / killing grace — all the pretty
Lil / sons & daughters killing not to be killed
Who will no longer hear the music just BOOM / BOOM / they will
Never dance again / read or write poetry and lose their sight
Of natures sacred landscape

War —what is it good for?   BOOM!

Weeping knows no borders / blood knows no borders / killing knows
No borders / death knows no borders

Where is Jesus / Allah / ask the people of the lie and they will lie
and lie and lie again and again 2X

War —what is it good for?   BOOM!

Inspired by Italian American poet Rosette Capatori

State of Emergency
9/11

blu-nite lite up the morning sky
w/unsettled passion exploding between
steel cobalt legs screaming
across the sun two long purple tears running down

the world trading time turning ashes of eyes
frozen across geographies slashing the air
like lightening while the sound of thunder
tilts the earth and the music above my head
turns to blood

crawling out of the burrows of this open
tomb doing an eagle-spread collecting
kneecaps and prayers, breathprints of the innocent
picking the pain like lint

sifting between the burning sand, loose bones
dream eyes & visions with an untamed pen
turns the bloodleaf pages to stone
woe unto the unholy souls

seize the season
to understand the love of hate
& the challenge
to turn hate to love

Thing Thang

we guard these things
things with no faces
things that collect dust in tight spaces
things that weigh us down
too soon fatigues our eyes / upsets our minds
things we have too many of / too much stuff things
we guard these things
things that can be thieved from us
burnt-up water-soaked
and gone with the wind
we guard these things
things that crack knees, hearts
and circles broken
things that stare at us blind and drive us crazy
we guard these things
we kill for these things / lie for these things
cry for these things
cut-up and act a fool for
w/ hearts unsung
children unstrung
love undone
its a thing thang
ying yang
bang   bang   bang

we keep guarding these things
only to die and leave these things ....

Dr. King

I.
He collected the eyes
Eyes snatched from between the legs of his ancestors
Eyes that floated on the waters sunstruck gold as yams
Turned bloody eyes that fell into the dust eyes that hung
From naked trees in the hush

He collected the eyes
Eyes w/ promise in an unpromise land
Eyes pregnant with dreams
Strung them like gospel pearls around his waist
He collected the eyes of his ancestors
The never to die eyes

II.
He saw the rapture beyond the rupture
Beyond the great divide and steel cobalt eyes
That lit up scarlet flames under purple skies and burned
The backs of the sons of the daughters of the delta
Beyond the licorice laments in the hush

He saw the rapture beyond the rupture
Beyond the back of the bus and the mississippi mud
Birmingham jails and lil girls smoke trail ribbons in the sky
Squeezing the waters out of a mothers wet heart and fathers
W/ hurt swollen too big for their mouths

He saw the rapture beyond the rupture
Beyond the cotton seed and sharecroppin
Shacks and concrete
Streets and marches and Cicero and Selma-hell-hounds
And Bull/ Big Bull w/ hog maw jaws and water hose

He saw the rapture beyond the rupture
He saw the mountain where the spirits gather and lips
Dripped w/ prayers circling the universe and saints knitting
Hands showing him a new land and visions talked back to god

He saw the rapture beyond the rupture
Beyond the BULLET ratatatatatatatat ....

The Second Coming

in memory of James Baldwin

You warned us Jimmy
You never spoke a word of lie

    the fire next / time

This ugly is knee / deep
All the dry-bones
The spiritsongs
Dusted over
Watered down
But not dead

You warned us Jimmy
The windreepers will come back
Unearthed
The rain-weepers have nomore tears
The seeds handsown have comeback bloody
There is no harvest

You warned us jimmy
Warned us w/ the word
You taught us how to dance with the rage
That it is not in the wrestle or the fight
But the fire and the dance
The firedance, the holy dance
The footstomper's feet burning
Purifying and getting / ready dance

    the fire next / time

You warned us Jimmy
Of the second commin
But we got to busy / too hi
Too busy
W/ these worrisome bluz for mr. charlie
Too busy
On the imitation of this nation

Too hi
Mistaking the chaos above our head for the muzic

We didn't hear the singing stop — change key
And turn to talking

We got too busy / too high
We got too busy / to hi

Rivers of Women

The Women Gather

The women gather
like painted brides/ a tapestry
of eyes/ hands/ knees/ hearts like open baskets
pieces of their peace/ fragments of their dreams
snatches of their lives/ with their mothers
mothers rhythms/ visions/ breathprints/ wrapped in their bosom

The women gather
dropping tongues in terra-cotta bowls
with their bibles and charms/ bluz, boogie, herbs, oils, and curls
seeing eyes and gospel pearls/ heady laughter/ lies and tears
rolling like Jordan/ prayers, rituals, and folktales
stuffed between their teeth/ a bloodline rich and mahogany

The women gather
mothers, daughters, sisters, wives, and sweethearts
grannies and aunt sister bell and hoochies with their hellhounds
and hollars/ their children and men/ lost lovers/ lifted
leftover/ forever and lasting with skeletons/ secrets/ gri-gri
and hush-hush folded in little bitty pieces

The women gather
knitting hands/ re-stitching their lives
reconnecting the circle
piecing the quilt to keep us warm
from generations for generations and generations to come...

(For Jayne Cortez)

From the tabernacle of poets — she tongues
A rhapsody of fire / burning the veil
Exposing the alabaster people of the lie
Rapping mahogany lips around a saxamony sonnet
Harmonizing / black redemption / the kingdom is come
The blood of strange fruit / resurrects you
Be bold / be brave / be wholly free

Rivers of Women

I HAVE KNOWN WOMEN/RIVERS OF WOMEN
blu/blck/tan/high/yella/blu-vein women/rivercrossing women/waters
deep as the nile/mississippi as mud/seaboard and island ocean
women/women who ride the waves and balance the tide/swimming
women/waterwalking women/treading waters/floating/going w/
the flow women/backstroking/jellyfishing/mud crawling
women/i know women who drown/sinking women who sleep
at the bottom of the waters

I HAVE KNOWN WOMEN
flying women-hawkeye and eaglewing who spread/stir the nest/
strike the wind and soar/women who strap mercury around their
ankles/making airborne feet/flying women who fly off the handle/
up against brick walls and breakwing/women who fly non-stop
w/earlobes/elbows/toenails and tongues like flying saucers/fly
by night women swiftwing and blind as a bat at high noon/
straighten up and fly right women/women with magic
underwing/i know women of wonder w/moon eyes

I HAVE KNOWN WOMEN
bold/brave/brass and sassy women/cinnamon breath and whispering
smiles/women w/ custom designed life lines that make beauty a new
face/women w/struggling wrists/jagged edges/women w/life
lines that read like worn-out road maps/i know women sweetbread
and sourdough/rainbow wrapped

I HAVE KNOWN WOMEN
women who see/who lay a 3rd eye on evil dare it to move and make
it sink in a blink/women who hear/who put ear to a stone/
x-ray a moan/hear a cry before a tear drops/women w/ keen nostrils
who smell shit before it stinks/women reminiscing and ruminating
on the rudiments of roots and the source of natures remedies/
diviners/root women

I HAVE KNOWN WOMEN
troubled women w/ sacks/satchels/bags and bundles of trouble
women who serve trouble on a platter and chaos for desert
women who carry trouble like a bone/ w/ tall tales and who shot
john about other women/lying women/women who sneaky pete

at the backdoor and cheat in the frontroom/see sawin/hem-hawin/
double-tongue/lying women/thieving women who steal
your money/your honey and unlaugh your funny

I HAVE KNOWN WOMEN
women peachcheeks/maybelline/ruby lips/
swingin hips/face in paint/full of haints/women who sleep in your backpocket/
wear you down to a nub/run you ragged as sauerkraut
women who dare "DO RIGHT" to come round their stoop and make
"GOOD STUFF" tuck tail and haul ass/I know women who turn
peace to piss and put a hellhound at risk

I HAVE KNOWN WOMEN
dancing women/be-bop and shushu feet women who re-bop
a jitterbug real sweet/package a hukka-buck and sell it/
hip-hoppin/bop a boogie woggie stompin women/women holy
rolling/dancing w/ jesus/two stepping w/ the devil/rocking w/ the wind
women/drumfeet-bare and sturdy/dancing women
dancing the wrinkles out of their brows/bed and their head/
making spirit rise/passion/snatches a jellyroll and a boody-grind
like an electric slide women who point ballet/ boogaloo/dance
the nutcracker between the cracks-in her life

I HAVE KNOWN WOMEN
healing women/spirit women/of vision/women who beat a dream comin
true/peacekeeping women sun-sipping/women who light up dark corners
and dingy hearts/women who put a move on the fog/knees of harmony
and smooth teeth/divas and doers/righteous women of purpose/substance/
w/ music/wordwalkers between the foot of the mountain and the mouth
of the sun/lovesowers and seedplantingwomenbirthing and bridging/praying
women/standingground women/traveling light/ w/ good vibes laughing
   women
who be merry w/ tears that turn crystal/i know these women
these mothers and daughters and lovers and wives/these sisters/
   grannies/queenies
and hoochies/these women who make women to make women/to make men/
I know these women

I HAVE KNOWN WOMEN/RIVERS OF WOMEN
blu/blk/tan/high-yella/blu-vein women

knitting hands / collectingeyes / ribbons / photographs / hairclippings
poems and stories / stringing pearls and parables / tears and smiles /
gathering picnic baskets / silk gloves / birthmarks / teacups and ashes /
pickin the flowers / snatching the breathprints of women past / writing
a song called — WOMEN / RIVERS OF WOMEN

When a Sisterwomanpoet Prays

She prays w/ a glass eye
Sees double w/ single vision
Connects chains of light

When a sisterwoman prays
Muse and meditate
Fuse spirit and soul
Collects the higher power

She strips doubt naked
Kicks fear in the ass
Assassinates evil
Turns insight out

She touches the all-sum of god
Releases ego/transcends/expands
Breaks bread w/ the universe
The artist paints her angel

When a sisterwoman prays
She be gettin results

Broken N' Parts

For the women of the Montclair, New Jersey workshop, 1998

across bloodline and geography
the women gather / coming in from their winter
threads of yesterday's fabric
like a tattered dress that once
danced a full circle /
they come
w / tongues stuffed in their pockets
stories and tales swimming in the pools of their eyes
smiles of the lie / songs sleeping behind the mask
tears dried-up / dirges of lost grandmothers / fathers
who wore them like briefs / daughters who broke out of their mothers
womb running / sons who forgot to remember them / ditties
and dirges whispering under their skin /
they come
pieces of their lives balled up
in their fist / fragments of their dreams /
their houses / photographs / broken hearts and china /
fingernails like frayed paper flowers
they come like broke down promises
once firm breast fallen / the smell of love like
clabber milk / their rapture ruptured
they come
collecting shadows
picking up eyes and breathprints
that hang over their shoulders / coming
like a march wind breaking
against their backs
like the sun creeping thru the cracked skies
spirits rising from the ashes
they come
picking memories from b'tween their teeth
tracing the trail of their tears
and once upon a time laughter
rediscovering their voices
reinventing themselves
fresh dancing
busting loose / breaking bread
and silence / tale spinning and

story swapping/ shaking the wrinkles out of their tongues
piecing and patching/ reconnecting their broken circles
w/ healing threads
they come
full circle

We Be Dolly's Girls

We be Dolly's girls
Silk, sassy w/ good sense & classy
Love passed down in the bloodline
Rich like pot-liquor

DOLLY'S GIRLS

We know how to shine fine like elderberrywine
We know how to laugh, smile, cry and scream
Act dignified, uppity, sometimes grumpy
Act-up and out, in and out, country and citified
A little-bit crazy, a little-bit sane
Mix it all up, mix it all down with a dream and wish
We be a special dish, the bold, the beautiful, the brown
Some short, some tall, some skinny, others a little too round

DOLLY'S GIRLS

We know how to boogie with the boogieman
We know how to stomp with the devil
Sing with Angels with/out a cracked note
We know how to beat them odds — dance with God

We be Dolly's girls
Love passed down in the bloodline
Rich like pot-liquor

BLESSED/ REDRESSED/ AND/ FREE
A REFLECTION OF HER
LOVE-SUPREME

Sistas

We have sang / solo / duo / trio
cried / moaned / lied and laughed
      together

We have done the cat-eye
scratch in the night
holler'd / screamed like
a snaggle-tooth hyena
and fought like fire and woke-up
in the smile of a new sun
      together

We pieced together our dreams
witnessed stuff fall apart at the seams
kept sacred our secrets / being who we be
earned degrees / helped each other in dis-ease
choked back life's tears / untangled our fears
fell down busted-up and scar'd our knees
got up and started all over again
      together

Crashed hormones and tracked hellhounds
witnessed the miracle of birth touched
the pain of death and the ugly of sick
felt the beauty of god's spirit
been redeemed, been born again
      together

Tasted love and loss and memories
felt the cooling board of our mother
the winding sheet of our father
and the smootheyes of each other
      together

Discovered our beauty / our strong / our talents / ourselves
we are love-rich and mahogany / we are friends
we are sistas

Daughters

you have been my sunshine
my rain, good nuz and my
cloudy day

you been my stories
my morning-glory, my
song, my dance, my prayer
two tears runnin, my

pride and joy, heart
unstrung, a trouble/beat
a peace to keep, a reflection
of me, a love supreme

you be the poetry of my poems
my sisterladywomangirls
a daughter's love ain't got no

    END ....

Illumination

A tribute to Alice Coltrane

With long enchanting fingers she kisses the deep blue
lips of sound melting into every string/strumming
the stubborn past/painting the future with a righteous
brush/connecting the magic of wind in sync with shells
singing to the sea

Plucking the breathprints of life from the open mouth
of god/weaving a new language / born of the ancient spirits
in a natural key / a C sharp ear stringing melodic pearls
around a time of impatient chaos / breaking the voodoo/
healing the dried-up wounds of the unloved / understanding
the nuance of a moan / turning the tears of the bluz people
into the laughter of rain

O'Black Orchid / Empress of strings
we hear the music / like the proud spread of a peacocks tail
the Gullah of the drum with Kori chants like the sweet bird
of paradise / humming to the soul of the butterfly / the honey in the rock
of ages / the lyrical lyre/ the voice of water dancing with a chorus of trumpets
obos and violins composing a cello song /

We can hear the music / flutes and kazoos
soothing the fly's flicker / the babies swimming in the womb / the men
who cry in silence in unison with a smothering cricket / like
rainbows and lightening flashing in our blood / running in the knees
doing a plie / a crescendo orchestrated from the rolling hills of eyeballs
echoing god's voice n' harmony n' balance

We hear the music / Alice / Empress of strings with the sound
of a love supreme / you have moved us to the edge of the world
a global gospel / where we discover ourselves / a new language

the sacred art of the harp / threads of light
we feel you in the ear of our heart

ILLUMINATION

My Soul Look Back in
Wonder 'How I Got Over'
for Mahalia Jackson

I woke-up this morning
More than something on my mind
Woke-up
Under a New Orleans sky
Raspberry dust crawling the green
Where clouds sweat / blossoms scent sweet
Voodoo walks and a mojo talks where
Cooling boards like wooden hands lay slavery drybones
Wrapped in black winding sheets / someday to rise again
W / nommo swansongs or dirges black and blue
I woke-up

Woke-up w / more than something on my mind / me-jesus-chicago
Got out my traveling shoes
Woke-up / ready to MOVE ON UP A LITTLE HIGHER
Unhitched my mule / strapped on my gospel boots
Bus ticket in my hand / freedom spiritpraise in my bosom
The gift of song in the throat of my soul — don't you know
Harmony unstrung and a melody unbent / going up yonder
God made me song / and bid me sing a lift everyvoice song
A borned again song / my hope built on nothing less
Than faith and righteousness
I woke up / w / more than something on my mind / me — jesus — chicago
God made me song / bid me sing
The Amazing of God's Grace
Soon one morning I put on my traveling shoes
To walk all over this land
From the Mississippi bottoms
To England's kingdoms

God made me song / made me free to sing
Uplifting the lowly / humbling the boldly
I woke up this morning / the song
God song / a peace song / a gittin up song / a love song
I woke up this morning singing / singing / singing
And
MY SOUL LOOK BACK IN WONDER 'HOW I GOT OVER ....

Dame Dunham Dance

She comes from the sage garden
With the rhythm of Mutima dancing under skin
Whispering breathprints out of Africa / spirit songs
Singing under the soul of her feet
Drum voices speaking in mahogany tongues calling
Nations of talking feet / river dancing spirits
Choreostories reconnecting our bloodline in black gold

Time/Wise
for Me Me

She saw tomorrow
N/time-woman / time-mother / time
Like her mother's mothers before
Mother Mary

She saw tomorrow
W/a righteous eye / an ear w/an echo and a 7th sense
She cd see the sunrise in the sparrow's eye
Hear day-light fall into the arms of night
Feel the moon creep up and rescue the dark
She saw tomorrow
N/time/woman time / mother time

She knew time
Like she knew Jesus
Like she knew Joshua and her 13 babies

She knew time
She cd feel it
Like the long dark fingers of her ancestors
Feel it like dusk breathing a hush hush

She knew time
She cd smell it / smell it like trouble
Like a fresh storm brewing

She knew time
She cd taste it / like the honey in a woodwater rock
Like the red-clay in the bottoms that she dusted
Her lips w/now and again

She knew time
Like the inside of her palms
Like the leaves that settled in her teacup
Like the crystal in her children's eye
Like the fear in her man's sweat

She knew time
W/ every seed she carried and everyone she buried

W / every ear she pierced and every strand of hair
She cut on the new moon

She saw tomorrow
N / time seeing-eye time
Like the signs

She knew
The peculiar witchcraft of oppression like
The terror of a scream wrapped tightly in a sigh
On the secret of a moan / a prayer w / out a word

She knew
Life's only promise to be death and struggle's
Greatest invention to be victory

She knew time to be a matter / of / time
That all be appointed by time
That ungodly deeds would be done in the name of god
That freedom like truth / crushed / wd always rise
That the tears of the unloved wd come back / turned to blood
That the innocent like the guilty wd have to drink
That rage be the broken mirror of peace

She knew time to be a matter / of / time
That unholy institutions to be unnecessary to be holy whole
That the vanity of man's law to be lawless
That man like the monkey wd cut shines and capers
Footslip and be swallowed by folly and eat dung like hamburger

She knew time to be a matter / of / time
She knew time like the wind changes but never cease
Breaking out & up & clean for good smelling
That time to be different from times
That religion to be different from righteousness
That every spirit is not spiritual

She knew time like the wind changes but never cease
She knew
That man wd try to hold time / try time / record time / mark time /
Change time / ignore time / try to fold time in little bitty pieces

But time like the mind changes but never cease
Time   Time   Time   is just a matter / of / time

She saw tomorrow / n' / yesterday
N' time / womantime
Like her mothers / mothers / mothers
B'fore her mother Mary

She was like time stubborn & unmovable
A heritage
Singing in the bloodline — like gospel
A revival
Passing down time / rich like pot liquor
She was spirit / was time / was song / was poem
Healing — mending the circle
& like motherearth
Can't no grave hold a seeing-eye-spirit / time / womansong

Wildflowers

A flower grows / in beauty wild
seed of nature's soul / wildflowers grow
heaven's tears and sunstruck skys /
wicked winds / a breath of storms
under winters' gray or autumns' raspberry clouds

A flower born / laughs, lives, dances, sings, dies
returns / blossoms / again lives
nurtured by nature

B'tween green weeds and sweet grass / meadows
and fields / clover and brush like a woman tale
spinning her colorful journey swirling and
skirting pinksweets and poppies / primrose and
buttercups / chamomile and chicory / blu flax and
baby breath purple cones dandelions and daffodils /
catchflies and a dragon fly among a basket of
gold (marigolds) / /   Nurtured by nature

Wild as blackeyed suzies / scarlet yarrows, morning
glories / wild blu iris / Johnny jump-ups / ox-eyed
daisies soothing as lavender hyssop and creeping
zenias growing wild along roadsides and byways
highways / country trails and iron rails
                    Nurtured by nature

A colorama spray growing / beauty wild like
a ladywomanflowergirl / bending / swaying / face-up
and bowing / standing tall in the earthtones
and greens in chaos and calm / growing
                    Wildflowers.........

Poem for a Black Woman

I house the legend of Mutima
The heartbeat of the earth
I am the offspring of the moon and the sun
Thrust from the energy of Africa
I am the Black Woman

I am the symbol of love
The channel of creation
The vibration of peace
The anger of storms
The pain of suffering
I am the Black Woman

I have seen the first rain
And the last fire
I am the seasoner of souls
I have many tales untold

My womb has been stretched
across the mouth of the universe
To create rhythms and nations
My body has borne witness to birth
My spirit the taster of death

I have seen the 13th month
The 32nd day
The year 3000 before the year 03

I have cradled the newborn's cry
Yours and mine
Collected the old man's moan
Made diamonds out of stone
Found gold in my soul

I am the right hand of God
The equal part of Man
The spirit of Life
I am the Black Woman

NATURAL TO THE BONE !

Rituals

Healing

Bear my wind cracked song
Wounded on the second bar
In the throat of your silver trumpet
Play me a getting up morning
A full heart melody
Fold my brokenwing inside your bosom
With a healing score
Dance me upstream
A golden salmon sonnet
An angel overture
On a long silk-tome
Make the music honeysweet
A clear note
And let me soar...

Son-song

I came humming rich and mahogany like
The healing sap of the eucalyptus in my
Grandmother's hand

I came to make you joy w/ the innocence of my childhood
To let you taste the proud of my youth and let you catch
A glimpse of my manhood / giving you pearls of memories
To grow into the wise of your aging

Now I am rising, stripped of time and space
Passing into the twilight / to wake into another sphere
To sing above your head / to dance on untrodden fields
I am rising circling the seasons unbroken
I am rising, my love wrapped around you
No hand can erase
I am rising

The Sonsong/ the Spirit Song/ God's Seed/ a Love Supreme
To be ever more near to thee...

The Wedding

We come/ pouring the libation / resurrecting the eyes
Of our ancestors / collecting our bloodline
Retracing our beathprints
Breathing a whole-note
Giving wings to our heart
Creating a love song / to dance
In praise of the sacred / You & Me

Laying our wedding wreath
Embracing a band of gold & raspberry orchids
On the breast of a smooth stone
Drinking the jasmine air / wrapping
The magic of the sun around our ankles / stitching a new covenant
Under the souls of our feet
Knitting hands/ the light of a la la poem
Wrapped around our shoulders

Consecrating this day in the newness in the nowness
Laying the foundation of our union / stringing our laughter /
Our joy / Our visions / Dreams / And the crystals of our faith /
Our hopes like a rope of pearls / to tuck
Away in a tiny silver box / tied w/ scarlet ribbon
Anointed with God's tears and a slender prayer
To open
In our dry seasons / when midnite drops a blu/ spot
And storms come courting /
To be refreshed / renewed / reclaimed / and keep us comfort
When gray makes a silver nest in our hair

We come
Together... Making our memories... Painting our future
This day

Color Me Love & Sing
dedicated to my parents

In the season of your silence
In the hour of your twilight
You have become — full bloom

To drink of God's eye
Transformed / redressed, released from all distress
You have come full bloom

With hands stretched skyward, where the eagle stirs
And the angels hold a welcome feast
Singing you a homecoming song — a sweeteye melody
A harvest hymn
To celebrate your rest, your freedom
Where you are bountiful and boundless
With no sting, no grave, no swansong
Just lift your voice
Sing with the saints in exaltation

Sing the amazing of God's grace
For you have finished the race
Know that the holyspirit unfolds
All the reason and wisdom

Take up your lute, your tambourines
Make a joyful noise
Sing free — we will hear you in the soft hum of spring
Whistling thru the holy grass
Sing free — and plant a kiss
On the first rose of summer
Sing free — we will see you in the raspberry skies of
Autumn and the rustling leaves of color
Sing free — we will feel you in the brisk breath of winter
Watch you dance between the snowflakes

Lift your voice create your homecoming song
For when age finds us, your beloved
And dusk clouds whisper and storms visit
Like time, love, sunshine and God — a reflection of light
You'll be our lovesong

Always circling around us
And *like the sparrow* — You'll be watching us
Your children and your children's children's children
For generations to come

> *In the melody of silence*
> *mine eyes drink from the*
> *quiet stream / in search of*
> Peace

Echo of the Heart

Celebrate the melody of my quiet, my still, my rest
Make a joyful noise / for me
Clap hands, let the spirit of the Lord come down / for me
Light a candle
Hush a lullaby
Make a prayer
Sing a love-song / for me
That I may keep my rest
That I will be blessed
Now that my spirit is free of this restless sea

Touch the crystal in your tears
And you will find your rainbow
All is well w / me
Let rain wash the scales from your eyes
And bring you understanding
Watch winter's breathprints disappear
And bring you wisdom
All is well w / me
Life is the fountain of our chaos and our peace
God, the magician of healing

I walked and talked, laughed and cried
Amongst you / with you / for you
Now my spirit dances with the mystery of death
Life's greatest invention

Let my good-days be your keepsake
May the sun wrap arms around you to keep you warm
Keep me a priceless gem in your heart
Etch me precious in your memory
Celebrate the melody of my quiet, my still, my rest
All is well w / me
Like the sky, the mountains, the rivers and wind
I will always be with you
Remember me, a quiet step

Wedding Poem II

They gather from across geographies / family and friends come
to bear witness to this your day of consecration / your union
here and now celebrating yesterdays newness that gave birth
to now / creating your own love song that mirrors your commitment /
your trust / your hopes and vision / a communion
sonnet that illuminates two souls of one spirit / a sacred dance

This day lay your love wreath blessing your tomorrows unborn
pledging your love with pinksweets and lilies / raspberry orchids / hyssops
and sweetgrass / morning glories and clover baptized with the jasmine
air sealed with a gold band / stitching a new covenant under the soul of your
feet sunstroke smiles praising the rapture of this ritual anointed
by the breathprints of God and the crystal tears of the angels like a raindance

This day wrap these precious memories / the joy of your laughter and
the gathering of doves / the solidarity of the peace / put it in a shiny
silver box tied with a scarlet ribbon kiss it with a love prayer to open
in your dry season / when storms threaten and mid-day seems like
mid-nite to refresh you, to comfort you / restore you, smooth out the wrinkles
even when nature makes a silver nest in your hair and remind

Yourselves / your journey together / remember the magic of this day
a Love Supreme when you promised to be
we together / before the gathering
a symbol of God's Harmonic Convergence

Breathprints
for Barbara

Light a candle for me
Say a prayer
Whisper me into the wind
Lay a love wreath on the alter of your heart
And remember my good days amongst you.

God let down hands
Touch me in the wee hours
Just before dawn / preparing me / for a new sunrise

God called me
To the healing stream / like a balm in Gilead
Bathed my pain away
Gathered my breathprints / collected my heartbeat
Took my spirit on high / gave me new eyes
Rearranging my time / and like a sweet chariot
Swinging low to carry me gently home
All is well with my soul.

Weep if you must / it is good to unburden your tears
But make brief your grief / let the joy of my laughter
Comfort you
My spirit will be the music above your head
My love like the wind beneath your wings
To lift you in your weary times / so you may see
The sunrise
All is well with my soul.

Just remember
I am dancing with Angels
Celebrating my New Life.

Rider of the Tide
from the heart of Jimmy

I have crossed over into the hush
To soar like the eagle to the mountain
Enroute to rest in the soular of the sun...

Lite a candle for me
Lay a love wreath with my name under the magnolia tree
Play me a sweet groove melody like the breathprints
Of the wind / say a prayer if you wish
Embrace my passion for life and my days with you

      and remember my spirit

One tender in heart and tough in mind
My dreams that made my reality / one of few words and much action

      remember my spirit

How I danced with life's brassbones and rainbows
My love for my family and my children and my ole dog Jake,
My humor, my hobbies, how I loved you all because I loved myself
Looking good and feeling fine / stuff the precious of me in
Your pockets and know like the rider of the tide, I lived my
Life unencumbered and *I Did It My Way*

      just remember my spirit

Now let this day of my parting be the day of your gathering
Knitting hearts & hands — lift your voice celebrate me
Tell my story, pass me down thru my children and grandchildren
Who made me proud to be called dad and even more proud to be
Originally named Brand-Dad by Julian. To them I say stay
Strong / stay beautiful / work hard and enjoy your life   but

      remember my spirit

At the closing of my pages I leave with you my heart saying

Weep today / crying is healing like crystals
But tomorrow hang your tears out to dry

Have no regrets of yesterday
Pick-up yourself/keep my love close to you
And with grace as amazing as God's eye on
The sparrow, I'll be watching you......

The rider of the tide, Big Jim/Big Daddy/Branddad.

For Minnie Alberta Parron
(1916 – 1991)

In the silence and tranquility
we drink from the eye of god — the healing stream
our spirit redress
to share in the light of a newday
to be given in marriage to the sun
embraced by the peacemaker of soul
given the gift of life-ever / and / lasting . . .

Take up your lute and sing me
The ripe fruit not given to falling
Instead, in patience waiting to be handpicked

By the master / artist

To join the flow in the bend of the river
Handstretched skyward, where the eagle stirs
And the universal choir chants in unison

All praise be unto the creator

Take up your lute and sing me
A morning glory easy like evening prayer
A deathless praise, a sweeteye melody

A spiritsong

That will always hold in your bosom
To celebrate my quiet, my still, my rest

Sing me blessed

Free as the music you hear in the hush
I am your harvest hymn, your reaping tree

Take up your lute and sing me

Bountiful, Beautiful, boundless / free
No sting, no pain, no grave — all is well w / my soul
For in the grace of my season / is born your wise

Feel my love blot-out your fear
So you will know that I am to you even more near
Take up your lute
And sing me
Sing me / all of me
I too, am you.........

Transformation Transcendation
for LaGrande and Billie

I have come full bloom / ready for God's choosing / swing low the chariot
Lifting me up where I belong / taking my spirit on hi / an added ray
 of sunshine
Where the angels reign, preparing my welcome feast
I have drunk from God's eye the healing nectar
All pain undressed / released from all distress
I am renewed / transformed / transcending / bountiful, boundless, free
I have crossed over into the hush / to dance on virgin shores / among the
 water lilies
Blending my new voice with the universal choir
Where there is no sting / no grave / no swansongs
To sing the love songs with the universal choir / making music up
 above your head

        All Is Well With My Soul

Come my beloved ones collect my breathprints / knit your hands / your hearts
Celebrate my peace / my still / my rest / I have escalated / elevated
Take up your lute / your tambourines / lift your voices / make a joyful noise
Witness the amazing of God's grace / I have finished my race and
 honored my charge

        All Is Well With My Soul

I was sometimes the sunlight to brighten your haze
The hand helping to unwrinkle the maze along your way
The Lullaby that calmed & comforted
Like a sturdy oak I was your confidant and friend / making no complaint
For my children / a gentle smile that tried to understand somehow
W / unconditional love / spreading my love like butter on a proud piece
 of warm bread
Now my soul has opened up / I'm in the first realm of my rising All Is Well
N' the newness of the nowness / treasure the precious of my memories /
 lite a candle
Make your prayers / sing me a homecoming song / a sweet-eye melody

        This is my harvest

A Tribute to the Ancestors
Family Reunion (a ritual*)

We gather from across geographies
Collecting the breathprints of our ancestors
Together knitting our hands / a symbol of unity
A communion / in solidarity / family communion

Let us pour the libation
(pour from the white pitcher)

Let us lay a wreath of flowers
(lay the flowers before their image)

Now, Let us speak the name
(each speak a loved-one's name)

We do this in remembrance of our heritage
We invite their spirit / in honor of our bloodline

(for narrator):

Let us not forget to remember, the path of their journey
Their tears, their pain, their joy, their laughter, their gifts
Their psalms, their prayers, their songs, their visions, their dreams
Their struggles, their victories, faith and love
For it has been and is the foundation for our individual families
In the union of this reunion as their offspring's recommit
Ourselves as family / to love / cherish / forgive / and respect
Each other / continuing to pass on their strength and spirit
Of their living in this generation and generations to come.

In the words of the old African proverb be reminded:

We are because they were
(all)   I am because you are (Weusi)
And down thru the generations
We all are because of God

---

* *A table with a cloth cover holds the pitcher of water that is poured into a bowl. Each child lays a fresh flower on the table by the picture of a loved one who has gone, speaking their name.*

Family Re/union

gathering of tribes

'Rejoice and be glad'

We come
Gathering across geographies
Knitting hands/blending heartbeats
A melody in unison/ a harmonic convergence
Celebrating the breathprints of our bloodline
Stringing the gift of love like gospel pearls
Around our waist

We come
Making prayers and songs / laughter and merry
Collecting the wisdom of seasoned minds
And the innocence of new eyes / the spirit
Of those who have stepped over into the hush
Who like the sparrow keeps watching us

We come
Greeting the familiar / welcoming the new
Linking and bonding a circle of time
Standing in the face of grace
Gathering love / creating a sacred space
Refreshing us / renewing us/ restoring us
Together /

We come
This day / this moment/ this hour
Elevated to the 3rd power
N' harmony N' balance / you and me becoming we
For tomorrow's memory
Like a slice of fresh air / it's a family affair
You and me and us and we / celebrating who we be
A piece of our ancestral clan / touched by the light of angels
The gathering of a tribe / continuing to piece the quilt
Passing it on from generations to generations to come
Together / We Come / Blessed...

My Song for You
Dedicated to Fontella Bass

Lite candle for me
Lay a love wreath for me
Play on your lute a sweet melody
In unison with the breathprints of the wind
Sing a prayer / let your song circle your dance
In celebration of my days amongst you

Remember my spirit / my tender heart / my tough mind
My love for you our laughter and tears / stuff the precious
     of my memories in your breast pocket and
know I am always with you a love supreme

I have stepped over into the hush free from death's sting
And pain released joining the seasons in the rising of the
Sun on a bright spring morning, in the strawberry sky
Of autumn / you will feel me a cool breeze on summer
Day and when snow birds fly into the arms of winter

Let this day be your day of gathering knitting hearts and
Hands like a love quilt passing it on for generations
Reminding you to stay strong, stay beautiful

I remind you / weep today / crying is healing like the /
Beauty of crystals / but tomorrow hang your tears out
To dry for all is well with my soul for only when the
Caterpillar dies and the butterfly fly

Know like the grace as amazing as Gods eye on the
Sparrow, I will always be watching you ....

Drum

i cum
a hollow hemisphere
filled with the voice of your ancestors
my mouth is covered with their membrane

i am an extension of Mutima (the heartbeat of the earth)

i am drum
study my ways
learn of me
touch me
make contact with my spirit
and i will reveal
the secrets of time
the ancient language

i am drum
i call rhythm
possess your body
i command life
conjure history thru you
to echo
between the heavens and the earth
you are an extension of my torso

i am drum
i too am tree
i call rhythm
command the word
the source ritual

cum poets
praise-songsters of the word
dip your tongue
into the dark ages of my loins
and taste ancient secrets
be full with the knowledge
erected by the aged
you are emissary
word sorcerer

let your message be divined
by my voice

i am drum—
i too am tree
          am drum, am tree
                    am drum, drum, drum

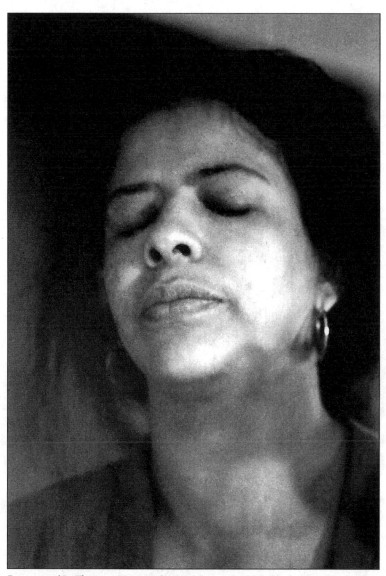

Portrait of LeFlore in Kansas City, MO, circa 1970. *Shirley Bradley LeFlore Collection.*

Oliver Lake and Shirley Bradley LeFlore performing circa 1970s. *Shirley Bradley LeFlore Collection.*

LeFlore with Toni Cade Bambara (seated) in St. Louis, circa late 1970s. *Photo courtesy of Sherman Fowler.*

Charles Wartts (left), Margaret Walker (center) and LeFlore (right) in Brooklyn, New York, circa 1980s. *Photo courtesy of Eugene B. Redmond.*

LeFlore (standing), performing with Fontella Bass (left), Zimbawe Nkenya (center), and Maurice King (right), circa 1980s. *Shirley Bradley LeFlore Collection.*

LeFlore in Woodstock, circa 1993. *Shirley Bradley LeFlore Collection.*

Spirit Stage performing in St. Louis. J.D. Parran (left), LeFLore (center) and Joan Bousie Duffs, 1994. *Photo courtesy of Adelia Parker.*

Painter Luigi Voltolini with LeFlore in Italy during a tour with Fontella Bass, circa 1996. *Shirley Bradley LeFlore Collection.*

From left to right: Eugene Redmond, Michael Castro, K. Kurtis Lyle and LeFlore performing in St. Louis, 1999. *Photo courtesy of Eugene B. Redmond.*

A formidable group of poets in Chicago. From left to right: Eugene Redmond, Gwendolyn Brooks, Haki Madhubuti, LeFlore and Sherman Fowler, circa 1990s. *Photo courtesy of Sherman Fowler.*

LeFlore with Eugene Redmond (center) and Maya Angelou (right), circa 1999.
Shirley Bradley LeFlore Collection.

LeFlore serving as co-host of *phatLiterature, A Literary TV Show,* honoring Gwendolyn
Brooks at the Langston Hughes Community Library & Cultural Center in Corona,
NY, broadcast nationwide, 2002. *Photo courtesy of the IAAS.*

LeFlore (left) with Cheryl Boyce Taylor (right) and a friend at the Cooper Gallery in New Jersey. *Photo courtesy of Michael J. Smith.*

A gathering of poets. From left to right: LeFlore, Eugene Redmond, Amiri Baraka, Sonia Sanchez, and Quincy Troupe, 2002. *Photo courtesy of Margie Hollins.*

LeFlore with Hamiet Bluiett in St. Louis. *Shirley Bradley LeFlore Collection.*

Hanging out at the Harlem Tea Room in New York. From left to right: Rosette Capatori, Bonnie Bowie, Dorothy White and LeFlore, 2006. *Shirley Bradley LeFlore Collection.*

LeFlore performing at Lindenwood University in St. Louis, 2011. *Photo courtesy of Kelly Revelle, Revelle Photography.*

About the Poet

PHOTO: Kelly Revelle, Revelle Photography

SHIRLEY BRADLEY LEFLORE is an oral poet/performance artist and re-
tired adjunct professor of women's and ethnic literature. She holds a B.A. in
Language Arts and Behavioral Science from Webster University and an M.A. in
Psychology from Washington University in St. Louis. She was a National Insti-
tute in Minority Mental Health Fellow (NIMH), and is the recipient of Missouri
Arts Council and CDCA grants.

An original member of the renowned Black Artists Group (BAG) of St.
Louis, LeFlore, who performed her poetry nationally and internationally, has
collaborated with dancers and visual artists, and worked alongside some of the
music giants of jazz, blues, gospel, spirituals and classical music. She has also
worked with woodwind virtuoso J.D. Parran, the New York City-based music
group Spirit Stage, and collaborated on Hamiet Bluiet's BBQ Band recordings.

LeFlore's poetry and writings have appeared in many anthologies and maga-
zines, including *Spirit & Flame, Anthology of Contemporary African American Poetry*
(1997), *ALOUD: Voices from the Nuyorican Poets Café* (1995), *Black American Litera-
ture Forum: Henry Dumas*, Vol. 22, No. 2 (1988), *Turn in the River: Celebrate Issue
for Gwendolyn Brooks* (1988), and *SHEBA REVIEW: Anthology of Missouri Women
Writers* (1987). LeFlore has served on the editorial board of *RIVER STYX: Literary
& Arts Magazine* (1975-1988). She was a producer of *phatLiterature*, a multicultural
arts literary series for The IAAS, where she presented the works of literary poetry
legends Gwendolyn Brooks and Margaret Walker. She was also featured promi-
nently in the critically acclaimed novel, *Wildflowers*, written by her daughter, na-
tional bestselling author Lyah Beth LeFlore, who is also producing her play, *Rivers
of Women*. *Brassbones & Rainbows* is LeFlore's first collection of poetry. ✦

About the Cover Artist

FRANK FRAZIER, a native of Harlem, is a self-taught sculptor, painter and collagist that currently hails from Dallas, Texas. With an art career that began when he was seven years old and spans over 50 years, Frazier is well-respected in the arts community.

While Frazier attributes his talent as a blessing from the Creator and his greatest influence, he also credits artists like Romare Bearden, Jacob Lawrence and Elizabeth Cattlett as his biggest artistic inspiration, with black history and culture a driving force behind much of his work. When he paints, he uses oils, acrylics, watercolors, pen and ink, charcoal and other materials.

Best known for his "Tribal Series," in which he uses bright colors and geometric figures to explore his Pan-African "community-of-family" philosophy, Frazier is currently working on a series of paintings on the civil rights movement. Besides working as a teacher, mentor and activist, Frazier's work has been featured in books, and film and television programs like *Waiting to Exhale, Coming to America, Frank's Place,* and *Bustin' Loose.*

Frazier's works have also been shown and featured in numerous museums and galleries, such as the African American Museum, Hempstead, NY; Armour J. Blackburn Gallery, Howard University, Washington, D.C.; Martin Luther King, Jr. Library, Dallas, TX; the Brooklyn Museum, NY; National Civil Rights Museum of Tennessee, Memphis; the Schomburg Center and New York Public Library; and the Corcoran Gallery of Art, Washington, D.C. His cover art, "Doo Wop Series: Those Sista's Can Sang" is a watercolor wash that fits magnificently with *Brassbones & Rainbows,* exemplifying Ms. LeFlore's work. ❀

OTHER BOOKS BY 2LEAF PRESS

2LEAF PRESS challenges the status quo by publishing alternative fiction, non-fiction, poetry and bilingual works by activists, academics, poets and authors dedicated to diversity and social justice with scholarship that is accessible to the general public. 2LEAF PRESS produces high quality and beautifully produced hardcover, paperback and ebook formats through our series: *2LP Explorations in Diversity, 2LP University Books, 2LP Classics, 2LP Translations, Nuyorican World Series,* and *2LP Current Affairs, Culture & Politics.* Below is a selection of 2LEAF PRESS' published titles.

2LP EXPLORATIONS IN DIVERSITY

Substance of Fire: Gender and Race in the College Classroom
by Claire Millikin
Foreword by R. Joseph Rodríguez, Afterword by Richard Delgado
Contributed material by Riley Blanks, Blake Calhoun, Rox Trujillo

Black Lives Have Always Mattered
A Collection of Essays, Poems, and Personal Narratives
Edited by Abiodun Oyewole

The Beiging of America:
Personal Narratives about Being Mixed Race in the 21st Century
Edited by Cathy J. Schlund-Vials, Sean Frederick Forbes, Tara Betts
with an Afterword by Heidi Durrow

What Does it Mean to be White in America?
Breaking the White Code of Silence, A Collection of Personal Narratives
Edited by Gabrielle David and Sean Frederick Forbes
Introduction by Debby Irving and Afterword by Tara Betts

2LP UNIVERSITY BOOKS
Designs of Blackness, Mappings in the Literature and
Culture of African Americans
A. Robert Lee
20TH ANNIVERSARY EXPANDED EDITION

2LP CLASSICS
Adventures in Black and White
Edited and with a critical introduction by Tara Betts
by Philippa Duke Schuyler

Monsters: Mary Shelley's Frankenstein and Mathilda
by Mary Shelley, edited by Claire Millikin Raymond

2LP TRANSLATIONS
Birds on the Kiswar Tree
by Odi Gonzales, Translated by Lynn Levin
Bilingual: English/Spanish

Incessant Beauty, A Bilingual Anthology
by Ana Rossetti, Edited and Translated by Carmela Ferradáns
Bilingual: English/Spanish

NUYORICAN WORLD SERIES
Our Nuyorican Thing, The Birth of a Self-Made Identity
by Samuel Carrion Diaz, with an Introduction by Urayoán Noel
Bilingual: English/Spanish

Hey Yo! Yo Soy!, 40 Years of Nuyorican Street Poetry,
The Collected Works of Jesús Papoleto Meléndez
Bilingual: English/Spanish

LITERARY NONFICTION
No Vacancy; Homeless Women in Paradise
by Michael Reid

The Beauty of Being, A Collection of Fables, Short Stories & Essays
by Abiodun Oyewole

WHEREABOUTS: Stepping Out of Place,
An Outside in Literary & Travel Magazine Anthology
Edited by Brandi Dawn Henderson

PLAYS
Rivers of Women, The Play
by Shirley Bradley LeFlore, with photographs by Michael J. Bracey

AUTOBIOGRAPHIES/MEMOIRS/BIOGRAPHIES
Trailblazers, Black Women Who Helped Make America Great
American Firsts/American Icons
by Gabrielle David

Mother of Orphans
The True and Curious Story of Irish Alice, A Colored Man's Widow
by Dedria Humphries Barker

Strength of Soul
by Naomi Raquel Enright

Dream of the Water Children:
Memory and Mourning in the Black Pacific
by Fredrick D. Kakinami Cloyd
Foreword by Velina Hasu Houston, Introduction by Gerald Horne
Edited by Karen Chau

The Fourth Moment: Journeys from the Known to the Unknown, A Memoir
by Carole J. Garrison, Introduction by Sarah Willis

POETRY
PAPOLíTICO, Poems of a Political Persuasion
by Jesús Papoleto Meléndez
with an Introduction by Joel Kovel and DeeDee Halleck

Critics of Mystery Marvel, Collected Poems
by Youssef Alaoui, with an Introduction by Laila Halaby

shrimp
by jason vasser-elong, with an Introduction by Michael Castro
The Revlon Slough, New and Selected Poems
by Ray DiZazzo, with an Introduction by Claire Millikin

Written Eye: Visuals/Verse
by A. Robert Lee

A Country Without Borders: Poems and Stories of Kashmir
by Lalita Pandit Hogan, with an Introduction by Frederick Luis Aldama

Branches of the Tree of Life
The Collected Poems of Abiodun Oyewole 1969-2013
by Abiodun Oyewole, edited by Gabrielle David
with an Introduction by Betty J. Dopson

2Leaf Press is an imprint owned and operated by the Intercultural Alliance of Artists & Scholars, Inc. (IAAS), a NY-based nonprofit organization that publishes and promotes multicultural literature.

NEW YORK
www.2leafpress.org